Enjoy the Gift of Organization

The Treasure of
Careful Planning

Written By
Donna Kauffman

Central Plains Book Manufacturing
Winfield, Kansas

The Treasure of Careful Planning:
Enjoy the Gift of Organization
Copyright © 2003 by Donna Kauffman

All Rights Reserved.

For more information:
Donna Kauffman
19151 Hobart Road
West Farmington, Ohio 44491
kauffman@myepath.com
www.djkauffman.com
1-440-548-5436

ISBN: 0-9722411-1-6

Printed in the U.S.A. by
Central Plains Book Manufacturing
Winfield, Kansas

To all my friends who are seeking to
find the treasure in careful planning.
May this book be an encouragement to you.

Acknowledgements

I am indebted to:

My heavenly Father for designing me by His hand, and leading me in a path of fulfillment.

Anne Ortlund who through her book Disciplines of the Beautiful Woman inspired hope and a future for me.

My helpful critiquers: Hope, Audrey, Mary Lois and Glen.

My editing group: Sharon, Verda, Ronald, Ruth and Jo Ellen.

My final, careful editor: Kristina.

My proofreaders: Bob and Kristina.

To each of you, I express my sincere thankfulness for your hours of capable assistance and wise counsel.

Contents

1

A Call to Minister

When our oldest daughter, Carla, reached the age of four months, we packed our belongings into a van. My husband, Bob, Carla and I traveled 20 hours north following the Lord's call to minister with Northern Youth Programs. Carla was 15 months old when I gave birth to Rachel, our second daughter. There in our quiet northern setting I encountered a bout of loneliness. Because there were only a small number of mission workers, I had few friends in my new setting. With family and acquaintances far away the realities of adult life loomed before me like never before. I realized I not only had a marriage to nurture, but two tiny daughters as well.

In the winter months in northern Ontario it gets dark very early. Each afternoon, I checked the clock while I wandered to the big living room window to pull the curtains, and shut out the darkness. As I drew the curtains, the thick blackness I was determined to seal out seemed to leap into my heart. I felt engulfed with solitude. Every day I turned from the window and dragged myself to the green chair that sat in the corner of the living room. Kneeling down beside it, I called out to the Lord to meet me, to touch me, to encourage my aching heart.

I wondered, *what* am I on this earth for anyway? *How* will I make my marriage work? *Is* there any way to raise these children for God and eternity? Numerous questions crowded my ever lonely existence. Soon Christa, our third daughter joined the family. Responsible for another person with an eternal soul, I wondered how I would cope.

During this time a friend came by with *a* book. *The* book that held just *the* right message for *the* hour for me. I latched onto that book *Disciplines of a Beautiful Woman* by Anne Ortlund. Each afternoon as all three babies slept on the living room floor around me, I sat in the rocking chair studying the mind of Christ. It was through this book along with searching the scriptures that the Lord touched me. He came into my heart and ministered deep into my spirit.

I learned those days the "all important" in this life is *God* and *people*—and connecting the two. I set out to understand from the Lord what groups of people I should minister to. Certainly I couldn't encourage everyone on this earth, for I had this house full of people that took most of my time.

The Lord revealed to me that He held the *ultimate* reason for my being here. I needed to make Him the first priority of my every single day, no matter what the cost. My husband came next in line. I was to care for Bob in a way that drew His heart toward God. Next were my three daughters. How important for me to spend my time nurturing these little girls to serve the Lord. Beyond that, when time allowed, I would reach out to and encourage people within the family of God. Lastly my unsaved friends needed to hear the message of Christ. The people groups I was to connect to God, were first my husband, and second my daughters. The Christian family and unsaved friends came after that. I have established my life according to these priorities since that day.

The Lord responded to my pleadings and queries. He revealed His purpose for my being on this earth.

My days were no longer filled with menial, monotonous, homemaking tasks that left me feeling unfulfilled. Recognizing the ministry the Lord had given me made my efforts blessed.

I was reminded in Matthew 10:42 that even a cup of cold water given in Jesus Name was as if I were giving it to Him. Each piece of clothing I hung up for my husband in Jesus name was as though I was doing it unto Him. With every diaper I changed and each meal I prepared, I was constantly reminded I was doing these jobs for the Lord.

> If anyone gives even a cup of cold water to one of these little ones, he will certainly not lose his reward.
>
> *Matthew 10:42*

During that time I learned that few people have the opportunity a mother has. I had four souls in my home 24 hours a day to influence for God. When I meet individually with someone in need, I may spend one hour a week or two hours a month with them. When I teach a Bible Study or lead a ladies meeting, my impact is generally not longer than an hour once a week, once a month or even less than that. I had my family, four souls with me daily, that needed challenged to new heights in the Lord. What an opportunity! I was thrilled with my purpose.

My new passion led me to search for depth and wisdom in the presence of God. I knew the Lord expected me to train my daughters well and love my husband with my whole heart. Enabled by the Lord's power and my desire to please Him, I was able to do these things.

I also made a strong effort to encourage one person in God's family each day. I continued praying for and reaching out to many unsaved friends. The early years of loneliness had slowly vanished. In its place I found new invigorated significance and focus. I am on this earth to minister for God's glory.

And in the end
it's not the years in your life that count.
It's the life in your years.

2

Defining My Purpose

*J*esus came with the goal to seek and to save that which was lost according to Luke 19:10. He had one purpose for being here, and He spent his entire life working toward that vision.

Each of us have been given a ministry to fulfill. "Take heed to the ministry which thou hast received in the Lord, that thou fulfill it." Colossians 4:17 KJV. This passage reminded me that I also am gifted with talents and abilities to use for God. I needed to give thought to these things, seek the Lord, and allow Him to use me in the greatest possible way to connect my people groups to Him.

Challenged to dream my wildest dreams in relation to the five groups of people I was to connect to God, I eagerly opened myself to hear from Him. A dream is something that carries you forward from day to day. It's a statement about what we envision for the future. It can be something we wish to be remembered by when we die.

As I share with you what the Lord shared with me, I invite you to open your heart to hear His message for your life.

I jotted down the five groups of people that concerned me in order of priority and began dreaming my dreams about each one.

> One of the deep secrets of life is that all that is really worth doing is what we do for others.
>
> *Lewis Carroll*

1. God
2. Bob
3. Daughters
4. Family of God
5. Unsaved people

I asked myself questions like: In relation to my walk with God, what do I want to accomplish by the time I die? What is it I want to see happen in my relationship with Bob? What do I want for my daughters' lives? How do I wish to affect the family of God while I'm on this earth? What are my thoughts about the people around me that do not know the Lord?

I began answering these questions by writing down two or three things under each of the people groups. Twenty years later this paper is still with me. I refer to it periodically to check how well I'm reaching my *life-time goals*.

Life-Time Goals

1. Relationship with God

   • Philippians 3:10 "That I may know Him."

•John 4:34 "My meat is to do the will of Him that sent me, and to finish His work."
•To walk with God as my friend. Moses and David were called a 'friend of God.'

These three ideas formulated what I desired in my walk with God.

2. Relationship with Bob

•That our marriage would be above average.
•That our marriage would not stagnate, but grow in intimacy.
•That our marriage would minister to and bless other marriages.
•Proverbs 31:11 "Her husband has full confidence in her..." and, verse 28 "...And he praises her."

As a married woman I longed for our marriage to be rich and growing. My passion was to become a woman of God that Bob desired to praise.

3. Relationship with my children

•To raise the girls to glorify God and to minister for Him.
•Proverbs 31:28 "Her children arise up and call her blessed."

Observing my dreams for my daughters lives written on paper, I recognized my hours needed to be focused on accomplishing these virtues. I became aware of my great need for the power and presence of God. I did not have time to waste or to wonder about my reason for breathing.

4. My church family

I sensed my dream surfacing about how I wished

to minister to the Christian family. I knew in the depths of my insecure heart that no one would believe this desire could be realized through me. I feared what others might think if they found my paper and read my aspirations. I wrote the following words in very tiny print, only legible to me, and I diligently prayed over them. A short time later the Lord began to unfold these goals in my life. I have been busy with them ever since.

> Seeing my goals in writing helped me decide what steps I needed to take to reach them.
>
> *Melodee Helms*

- To be an encourager to believers.

And in tiny print:

- To have a ministry in counseling and teaching women, leading them to a deeper walk with God.

Dream your dreams, pray daily about them and bless the Lord as He ministers through you.

5. The unsaved world around me.

- To be a testimony in public by being warm and friendly.
- Relate to the unsaved people in my world in a Christ-like, compassionate way.

I believed in my heart I could pass a smile around to everyone I saw. I knew I had the ability to ask, "How is your day?" and to share appropriately that I would be praying for them. When the Lord allowed me the privilege to relate closely to unsaved people, I desired to give them my heart; to be Christ in the flesh to them.

My *life-time goals* were completed with a few dreams listed under each of these people groups. It would be these people I would minister to as long as I walked this earth. When I looked over my lists, my purpose seemed invaluable and I poured my heart into working at it.

Yearly Goals

Once you've written your *life-time* goals, it's important to take the time to annually evaluate your efforts. Each year toward the end of the year, find a few minutes and a fresh piece of paper. List the five priority groups on your new page. Begin by writing two or three things you can do to work on those goals in the new year.

For example, *That I may know Christ* doesn't just happen in my life. Ongoing effort on my part is the only way for that goal to be accomplished by the time I die.

Priority 1. My relationship with God.

For a particular *yearly goal* I might write: to study through the New Testament, or maybe I'll decide on the Old Testament. There have been other times that I decided to do a specific study for my devotional time. Books and study guides have been useful tools. Some years I'll plan a passage of scripture I want to memorize as well. At times I've made a goal to stop what I'm doing two extra times each day to spend five more minutes in prayer. Setting the timer for 11:55 a.m. reminded me to quiet my heart with the Lord for five minutes at that time. Resetting it for 3:45 p.m. gave me five more minutes of prayer time before the girls finished school.

All of these things worked to move me toward my *life-time* goal of *That I may know Christ*. Dream your dreams as you sit in the presence of the Lord. Develop creative methods to draw closer to Him each year.

Priority 2. My relationship with my husband.

Do you know how many exciting things we wives can do to strengthen our marriage relationship? As you establish one or two specific goals to work on each year, you'll be blessed with how your closeness with your husband will progress.

One year I decided to work together with Bob to have a date once a month. It would be a time for just the two of us to run off to a park, for a walk or a picnic.

Some years I decided to write a note to Bob once a month or once a week. Of course it was important to determine which day of the month or week I planned to write it to be sure it got done. I've found it encouraging to list special ways Bob has blessed me by jotting them in little love notes.

When you use your imagination you'll find yourself full of aspirations that will enrich your relationship. However, be sure to start small. It's better to accomplish a couple of areas well, rather than neglect a long overwhelming list.

Nearly 30 years of moving ahead with my one or two *yearly goals* has connected Bob and I in just the ways I longed for. In retrospect those dreams seemed large and impossible. It was working at our relationship one day at a time that attained wonders. Our marriage has not stagnated. In fact, it's grown well beyond what I believed possible.

Priority 3. My relationship with my children.

This is a fun relationship to dream about. When we take the time to jot down a plan the blessings we give our children are innumerable. Putting the ideas on paper helps us not to forget what they are. It allows for working on each one in its time.

One year I decided to teach the girls the 'fruit of the spirit.' I wrote that on my *yearly goal* page along with the day I wanted to specifically focus on the fruit for that week. I studied the individual fruit and collected information. We had a great time learning the virtues that follow living out each one.

Another year, I chose to take one daughter on a date each month. Just the two of us went out. We were in full-time ministry when the girls were young so our date nights were planned as frugally as possible. Those memories are precious.

As a family we also wrote encouraging notes to one another. We worked on specific areas of need in each daughter's life every year. On Tuesday evenings we started family night. The written goals kept us alert to these things. When the girls were toddlers, I made a goal to spend 30 minutes each morning with them. I called it "filling their love tanks." They were more apt to play together nicely as I did my daily chores when their love tanks were full. I stayed true to this goal through the girls' school years.

> The purpose of writing inspirational notes is to build others up because there are too many people in the demolition business today.
>
> *Norman Vincent Peale*

The purpose for all of this was to help me accomplish my dreams. I wanted my daughters to glorify the Lord and minister for Him. I believed it was important to use each waking moment of the day in fruitful training. Today, I bless the Lord as I observe my daughters seeking godliness.

When we attentively tend to our homemaking duties like laundry, ironing and cooking, we are placing honor on our family. These jobs also play an important role in sharing holiness with them.

Priority 4. The body of Christ.

I feel enthusiastic about all of these priorities in my life. This ministry is to be done only after our husband and children are well cared for. As you thought-fully plan your days you'll find you have time to bless people outside of your home.

Try making this goal for one year. Each Tuesday, after your house is in order and you've spent your 30 minutes of quality time with the children, take five min-utes to phone a friend to give an encouraging word. Tell her something you learned from the Lord yesterday or this morning. Bless her as she begins her day.

Possibly every Wednesday on a particular year you'll prefer to write a note to someone that would ben-efit from a blessing. Get it ready to stick in the mail, or hand deliver it on Sunday morning.

Maybe you'll jot down a goal to take your child-ren each Thursday morning to visit an elderly person. Practice some scripture verses together and plan to share them when you go. As soon as your children can put three words together they're ready to begin hiding the Word of God in their hearts. In December I took my two-year-old grandson Kyle to visit Mary at the nursing home. He piped right up and said the parts of Luke 2 he had memorized. Little children quoting scripture or sing-ing songs ministers to elderly people in a special way.

I've written a dream on a particular year to start one Bible Study. Another year I aspired to begin the sec-ond one. For about three years Bob and I prayed about our vision to develop a parenting seminar. I put these goals on my prayer list and prayed about them. I will never cease to marvel at the way the Lord works! With the goal written, I remember to pray about it regularly and answers are the encouraging reward.

Priority 5. Our relationship with the unsaved in the world around us.

You know, I find everywhere we've lived, the Lord brings people into my life that need Him. My *yearly goal* in this area may include visiting one of these unsaved friends four times that year. I may write down to invite one unsaved family to dinner. One year I prepared a Christmas dinner for two couples who didn't know Christ. We hoped they'd listen to snatches of the Christmas story, and realize we cared about them when Bob mentioned their names in our mealtime prayer.

The Lord Jesus is always imparting kindness. Whomever we meet, whether we know them or not, a kind word or a warm smile speaks Christ.

> Commit thy way unto the Lord; trust also in Him; and He shall bring it to pass.
>
> *Psalm 37:5*

There you have it, a few of my ideas for *yearly goals*. These goal lists find their home in the prayer list section of my notebook. I pray over my goals on Tuesdays.

I need to remind you not to become discouraged if you only accomplish your dreams one-half of the time. Every effort toward a goal is growth, focus on that. Always remember if you don't get it done one day or one month, start over the next day, or the next. There are years that I may get my note written to Bob only six months of the year. But, hey, six notes versus no notes still encourages our relationship.

From your *life-time* and *yearly goals* your daily list of *to do's* is established. Anything on your daily work page unrelated to these five priorities needs to be removed. We are on this earth for two purposes, God and people and uniting the two. Remember that Jesus came with the goal to seek and to save that which was lost. He had no room for anything apart from that in His life, and neither should we.

My friend, I bless you as you get your Bible, notebook and pen. While you sit quietly before the Lord listen to Him speak into your heart about your gifts. Living out His purpose brings our greatest fulfillment in this life.

Lord, Speak to Me

Frances R. Havergal, 1836

Lord, speak to me that I may speak,
In living echoes of Thy tone:
As Thou has sought, so let me seek,
Thy erring children lost and lone.

Oh lead me, Lord, that I may lead
The wandring and the wav'ring feet;
O feed me, Lord, that I may feed
Thy hung'ring ones with manna sweet.

Oh fill me with Thy fullness, Lord,
Until my very heart o're-flow
In kindling thought and glowing word,
Thy love to tell, Thy praise to show.

O use me, Lord, use even me,
Just as Thou wilt, and when, and where;
Until Thy blessed face I see,
Thy rest, Thy joy, Thy glory share.

3

Life in My Notebook
Practical

*F*or more than 20 years, I've used a notebook for an organizational tool. I believe the Lord has led me through my careful planning. I feel I've accomplished more in my life than I ever would have, if I had remained in my previous disorganized state.

Do you have lists scattered everywhere? Before I had my notebook, I had lists fluttering in every room of my house. Here is an example of how I used to operate. During my time with the Lord I'd remember something I needed from the grocery store. I'd take a second to jot it down on a scrap of paper where I was sitting, or I'd write it in my prayer journal.

Later, while in the kitchen I remembered a phone call that needed made, I grabbed some paper and wrote that down. While tucking in the girls for naps upstairs, a few more grocery items came to mind. Completely forgetting the list I started during my devotional time, I began another list, on another scrap of paper, in yet another place in the house.

During those disorganized days, I often found myself floundering by imaginary *to do* lists in my mind. I hardly accomplished the many things I felt needed done. Finally, when I took a minute and found another scrap of paper, I'd scribble down what seemed pressing for that day. Frequently, I found there simply wasn't as much to do as I thought. Working down through the list completed it in a short time. Without the list, I would have struggled away the day.

> Take from our
> lives the strain
> and stress,
> And let our
> ordered lives
> confess
> The beauties
> of Thy peace.
>
> *John Greenleaf*
> *Whittier*

Some nights I went to bed with my thoughts whirling, trying to remember all the things that needed done the next day. The baby had an appointment at 10:00, and Bob needed something typed, I could not forget that. As the mental list lengthened I'd determine to leave it with the Lord, but my night was still restless as I prayed at each waking moment not to forget these details.

There were lists everywhere on tiny scraps of paper, in my faculties and yet, they were not around when I needed them. Then I learned about putting all my lists together in one notebook. It changed my life. Let me share with you some ideas about how to get a notebook started.

Getting Started:

Buy yourself a planner at your local Walmart or Family Dollar store. Make sure it's a looseleaf planner for adding and removing papers. Along with this, buy a Month-at-a-glance calendar, and a package of blank lined paper to fit your notebook. You'll want some sticky labels that will fit over the tabs on your tab pages in your notebook as well.

Remove all the preplanned pages from the notebook, discarding everything except the tab pages. You'll want to discard the prepared pages because your notebook is going to become *you*. Those pages aren't you. The tab pages are made of a heavier weight paper. They will be useful in putting your notebook together. Your planner will be carried with you everywhere you go, from the kitchen, to the living room, to the bed room, to the grocery store.

1. Calendar

Put the Month-at-a-glance *calendar* in the very front of your notebook. Everything gets jotted down on that *calendar*. Use a pencil, then you can change things as necessary without a messy looking page. Having your *calendar* nearby at all times is a time saver.

Otherwise, consider you are away from home without your planner, and you make dates with someone without your *calendar*. Returning home to your notebook you find your overscheduled dates requires phone calls for corrections and changes. That equals wasted time.

2. Daily Lists

Take one of your tab pages, stick a sticky tab label over top the tab and write *Daily List* on it. Add a stack of blank lined paper behind it. I find these blank pages work better for me than the pre-planned daily or weekly scheduling pages you can purchase.

At the top of the first paper put the day and date, (e.g. Friday 10/11). The next page will have the next day's date on it. Make several day's worth of daily list pages. Next, you'll start your list of *to do's* for the day.

- Devotions (always first on the list and done at the first best time of the day)
- Tidy house

- Thirty minutes with children
- Baby's appointment
- Ironing
- Phone calls
- Schooling

I like working down through the list, crossing off as I go. The crossing off is important to help me stay focused and get the jobs done. On an especially busy day, numbering my list proves to be very helpful. I have found when I work by lists, there are often spare moments later in the day to catch a needed nap or read an article.

Some days I can't get everything marked off the list. Remember we plan under the umbrella of "*If God wills.*" So in the evening, when I take several minutes to work out tomorrow's day, those leftover items get transferred to tomorrow or the next best day they fit into.

> Since time is the one immaterial object which we cannot influence— neither speed up nor slow down, add to nor diminish—it is an imponderably valuable gift.
>
> *Maya Angelou*

3. Phone Numbers

If you're like me you don't enjoy looking up phone numbers in a phone book. I have a page in this section reserved for *phone numbers* for our family numbers, church family numbers, Bible Study ladies numbers, community friends, long distance friends and businesses. There is even a page for Bob's important phone numbers. Bob doesn't use a planner, but he certainly does depend on mine. I have a page in this section with his important numbers on it. Bob has learned to flip there to get the number he's looking for.

4. Shopping

When I run out of anything, I jot it down here. If

you're a menu maker, while making next week's menus add your needed items to the list. I keep a stack of blank lined paper in this section, as well as in many of the other sections. With extra paper available, I don't have to scramble for it each time it's needed.

The last page of this section is my gift list. At the beginning of each year I write all the names of the people I'd like to purchase gifts for during the year. Throughout the year as I hear of or notice something someone could use I jot down that item under their name. This cuts down on shopping time when I'm ready to purchase a gift.

5. Miscellaneous

This is the last section in the practical part of my planner. This section contains everything that doesn't fit anywhere else. There are canning lists from last summer, as well as reminders for annual doctor visits. This is where I put my packing list for traveling and a list of Scripture songs. I also have a page in here for my storage tub numbers and a list of the items in each tub, as well as my daily routine lists.

When we learn to plan under the umbrella of *"If God wills,"* we move ahead allowing Him to lead us in the plan. The little verse in Proverbs 16:9 reminds me the Lord expects us to consider our days. "In his heart a man plans his course, but the Lord determines his steps." It's fine with Him for us to know what we're hoping to do today, tomorrow and next week. He will make changes to our plan as He sees best.

This completes my practical daily living lists in a nutshell. You'll need to determine what kinds of lists fit into your own life, and make your notebook the most handy homemaking tool you'll use. I believe this planner idea has the potential to organize your life, and provide you with more time in your day than you ever thought possible.

Ode to a Notebook

by Catherine Yoder

I keep my brain in a notebook.
It's handy lying there.

When I tell it to remember,
Ink's faithful to declare.

It holds my work and grocery lists;
Has room for daily prayers;

Records my goals, committees, tasks,
Those pesky plans and cares.

My "bright ideas" feel secure
In notebook's steadfast care.

This loyal notebook lessens fear
My memory is impaired.

I'd recommend my notebook
To other frazzled wives.

Its quiet power to organize
Improves our daily lives.

4

Life in My Notebook
Spiritual

⁊ his part of my plan-
er is very precious to
me. It keeps in view my objective of knowing God.

As God's daughter, loving the Lord is my first
reason for living. The powerful verse Paul declared in
Philippians 1:21 "For to me to live is Christ," has served
as one of my unwritten motivators through the years.
Regular time alone with the Father is completely essen-
tial for me to live a Christ like life.

I like to schedule my appointment with the Lord
at the first best time of each day. It's important for me to
be consistent with the time and place I do this, as well as
to have a devotional plan prepared. Daily searching the
mind of Christ invites the Lord Jesus into our every
moment's existence. We draw close as a result.

The next section in my notebook is:

6. Prayer List

Over the years I've often been asked to pray for others. Although I quickly respond with, "Yes, I'll pray for you," I've learned I need to write their name on the right page of this section. Otherwise I forget their desire for prayer and my promise to pray.

Years ago I had a lengthy list on a piece of paper stuck in my Bible. It listed names of people and concerns I wanted to pray for every single day. Each day as I met with the Lord that list seemed to go on forever. I often prayed over about one third of the requests, then either fell asleep or gave up. Getting up from my knees I committed myself to doing a better job tomorrow. Tomorrow came and the same thing happened. After sharing my prayer difficulties with Bob, he suggested I divide my list into days. I opted for it. I took my pen and paper and started separating that list.

> For the eyes of the Lord are over the righteous, and his ears are open unto their prayers.
>
> *1 Peter 3:12*

My prayer list now looks like this:

Page 1

The very first page contains a prayer written by Betty Scott Stam, martyred missionary to China. As she went to her execution, she left her baby in a tiny room nestled in blankets to be found by... she didn't know whom. Her willing commitment at all cost reminds me each day that I am the Lord's. I will serve Him as He desires.

> "Lord, I give up my own plans and purposes,
> all my own desires and hopes, and accept
> thy will for my life. I give myself, my time,
> my all, utterly to Thee to be Thine forever.

Fill me and seal me with Thy Holy Spirit.
Use me as Thou wilt, send me where Thou
wilt, work out Thy whole will in my life at
any cost, now and forever."

Betty Scott Stam

The next two pages are filled with items I want
to pray over more than once a week. I divided these up
so I pray for each three times a week.

Page 2
1. Monday, Wednesday and Friday

•Commit my family to the Lord spiritually,
physically and emotionally.

For many years this note has served as a reminder
to daily entrust my husband and children to the Lord. I
know He will give daily protection in these three areas
in His way.

2. Bob
I have listed several items under Bob's name that
I pray for him regularly.

•Wisdom in leadership.
•Protection from sin.
•Spiritual growth.
•Etc.

Our husbands face many temptations in a days
time. I was encouraged as a young wife to daily lift Bob
to the Lord. It's played a significant part in enriching our
marriage.

3. Girls, husbands, husbands-to-be, grandchildren
Praying over the following list for the *girls'*
and their *husbands'-to-be* for probably two decades has
reaped rewards. Following are the simple, but profound

words I've brought before the Lord for these important people in my life. I'm blessed today as I enjoy answers to these prayer items in double fold. I longed for them to grow to:

- Be respectful.
- Be godly.
- Be prayerful.
- Have strong values.
- Read uplifting books.
- Watch only appropriate videos.

We don't own a TV or a VCR. I couldn't imagine wasting a few hours time watching the kind of things available today. True to my style, I didn't want the girls involved in time wasters, nor unhealthy sights before their eyes. Earnestly I prayed through their teen years that their hearts would be tender toward wisdom. I prayed they would abhor the evil found in the media world. They meddled with this when they were away from home, but today all three have come back around. They are very selective, if deciding to watch a video at all.

> What do girls do who haven't any mother to help them through their troubles?
>
> *Louisa Mae Alcott*

- Listen to wholesome music.

I don't care for a wide variety of music. I love the old hymns of faith, and I hoped my girls would follow in suit. However, we did allow tapes in our home by a couple of groups who sang gospel music. The girls tried to bring in a few other tapes, but we sensored those and retrieved them quickly. When our daughters were away from home, they each tampered with a variety of music. I heightened the fervency with which I prayed. Several days ago I chuckled and rejoiced when Christa announced to me, "Mom, I'm going to get tapes from the gospel group you allowed us to listen to when we were girls. That is the strongest beat of music I want my children to know." I wanted to shout, "YES."

The list for my children continues with:

- Have marriages that honor God.
- Know contentment/gratefulness.
- Be spontaneous, yet controlled.
- Know God deeply.
- Have good friendships.
- Know selflessness.
- Be responsible.
- Minister for the Lord.

Each of these items held deep burden and desire for me. Praying over them for these many years brought peace to my heart and protection to my children.

Next on this page is *Self*:

4. Self

Ladies, I am a woman who struggles with the flesh. My will fights against what I know ought to be. I need the power and presence of the Lord continually before me. Praying over these requests for myself each week has wrought miracles in my life. I ask the Lord regularly that I would:

- Choose love to all people each day.
- See the best in people.
- Have a good attitude.
- Don't tear people down.
- Be filled with praise and contentment.
- Never despair.

My friend, do you ever despair? I am guilty of this. There are times I want to refuse to lead another Bible study. Other days I want to quit being a pastor's wife. Some weeks my heart feels faint with discouragements. I need to pray regularly for the Lord's grace, through His power, to guide me to never *despair*.

- To be bold and warm.
- To have an attitude of faith, trust and rest.
- To overcome self-condemnation and people-pleasing.

Daily I also like to pray:
- "Wherein lieth acceptance lieth peace."
That age old quote from Amy Carimichael that I need to remember each day. I need the Lord's strength to help me do this.
- Don't take offense easily. I can take offense so quickly. The Lord encourages us to not do that.
- Have a meek response to situations.
Meekness means quietly and humbly receiving what the Lord brings to me.
- "Be it unto me as you say."
These are Mary's words. I long to learn to accept circumstances as they come, even predicaments just as Mary, Jesus Mother did. Whatever you say, Lord.
- Give thanks every day.
To learn contentment, it's imperative for me to be grateful.
- Claim the power of the Lord's resurrection in my life to live above fear, worry, etc.
His power is available to me, the same power that raised Jesus from the dead, and with it I have been victorious over many difficult areas.

> The best way I know to face each day is to prepare the heart first thing in the morning.
>
> *Ravi Zacharias*

Page 3
1. Tuesday, Thursday, Saturday

- Parents
- Church leaders

I've noticed at times I can go through a whole week forgetting to pray for our elderly parents, and committed church leaders. This list reminds me to pray regularly for them.

Page 4
1. Tuesday, Thursday, Saturday

- Date   Request   Answer

I love this page. It lists answerable requests. My son-in-law's hired man was quitting. He would need a new one soon. I jotted down the date I learned about this under the *date column* above, the request under the *request column* and I began to pray. When the Lord answered, I marked a PTL with the date of the answer under the *answer column*.

Our daughter and son-in-law applied to an adoption agency for a baby four years ago. That date and request remain on this page—in confident trust there will be a PTL and answer date in the Lord's time.

A friend sent an email asking that I pray about a specific request for the next three weeks. I wrote that down and started to pray. When she gave me the answer I eagerly put that date and PTL in the right spot.

When this page gets cluttered with requests and answers, I transfer the unanswered ones to a new paper. The old page is added to the storage box in the garage marked **Answered Prayers**.

Some requests have remained on this page for many years. I found if the need wasn't written down I soon forgot to pray for that request. With it in this prayer section it did not get forgotten, and I prayed until I saw the answer. Other requests have been answered within a day or two.

My faith has been strengthened from this one simple part of my prayer list section. The large stack of papers filled with PTL's continues to grow. Our Lord keeps His promises.

Page 5
1. Daily lists

Monday	**Tuesday**	**Wednesday**	**Thursday**	**Friday**
Unsaved friends	Christian friends	Missionaries	Ex. family	Family
	Widows			

I write out the names of the *unsaved friends* I'm praying for on **Monday's** page. I also have written the names of the *Christian friends* I like to bring to the throne on **Tuesday's** page. When one becomes *widowed*, her name gets listed as well. I have dear widowed friends' names on this list that I've prayed for over several years. I can only imagine my need to be lifted to the Lord if that were me widowed. I continue to pray for these women. Under *missionaries*, I have the names of those whom I am praying for. Writing out the names of each one helps me stay focused on the person and the need.

One day, about a dozen years ago, I realized I had neglected to pray for our *extended families*. So, I listed everyone's name on my **Thursday** page to remember to pray for each one weekly.

Also I have written two or three *families'* names from my church under each day. That way each week every family gets prayed for in a special kind of way.

Page 6
1. Fasting Day

I like to fast one morning a week. I keep a list of deep concerns I pray over especially for that morning.

This prayer list section has encouraged my heart and prayer life for many years. All of these lists receive additions and subtractions along the way. I've learned I can pray for many things, in a little bit of time, with a few organized lists.

As I mentioned before though, goals or plans are just that. Some weeks I may get to my prayer list only twice. I know every prayer I pray, (with a prayer list or without) and every period of worship I experience means growth. It brings me forward in my dream of walking with God as my friend.

Prayer Journal

For many years, I've used a spiral notebook for my prayer journal. Writing is the best way for me to share the depth of my heart and to connect me intimately with the Lord. When I'm struggling to get my morning started in prayer I flip open my *prayer journal* and begin writing. I'm soon in earnest prayer. Writing keeps me alert if I'm extra sleepy as well. My *prayer journals* from the last two decades are kept in a storage box in the garage, labeled **Prayer Journals**.

> We need simply to sit still and open our hearts to the counsel of God.
>
> *Max Lucado*

I am a pen and paper person however, there are some folks who are not. Those people find it difficult to keep a notebook or to write their prayers. That's ok, the important thing is to find a way that works well for them.

7. Scripture

I love this section. Over the years the Lord has repeatedly ministered His Word to me. As a verse becomes special I jot it down here. Today I have pages full of Scripture. Whether I'm sitting in a doctor's office or waiting in the car for someone, turning to this section feeds my spirit. I never tire of reading through these special promises.

8. Notes

In this section I scribble down notes that hold

special meaning to me. These are notes that I never want to lose. If I'm in the car and hear a stirring comment on the radio, I write it down in this section, to be savored later. When the *notes* section gets full I take the pages out and type the comments up under the proper heading. I have notes and quotes on *tongue, faith, forgiveness, God's love* and *peace* to name a few. I file these away and pull them out when I'm struggling in a particular area or preparing for a lecture. I love having these thoughts available in a moment's time.

In this *note's* section I will also write a prayer now and then. If I happen to be away and waiting on someone it's a place to flip to quickly, and an easy way to keep my mind focused on prayer while in a busy environment.

9. Other sections in my notebook have to do with items that are valuable in my life. I have a *Writing* section where I jot thoughts that come to me that I want to write about as soon as there is time. I have a *Church* section. We have goals for the church in here. In the *Church* section there is also a list of verses I pray over for Bob while he is preaching, along with various other things. Being a Bible study leader for several groups I have a tab called *Bible Studies.* Those pages contain things I need for the different groups.

Remember this part of your notebook also needs to become *you.* What are your needs in your walk with the Lord? Possibly a few lists would help you to move ahead in that all important, vital relationship.

Anything you wish to remember for your life and ministries will be in safe keeping in your notebook. Notebookers carry their mind and life in their little black book. And when we get home from church or Walmart and realize we left it there?? we run straight back to pick it up!

*God's power is unleased when
God's people intercede.*

Max Lucado

5

Homemaking Routines

*M*y *homemaking routine* lists are stored in the *miscellaneous* section of my notebook. It's helpful to write out routines and lists to use in many areas. However simple these routines may be, they quickly become habits. They will take little time if they're kept up regularly.

Evening Routine
- Check collection spots (explanation following).
- Tidy everything before going to bed.
- Relax for 20 minutes with knitting, a magazine or hot shower.
- Check email and answer anything that can be done quickly.

•Go to bed at a reasonable hour with my husband.

If my *evening routine* is done well, my *morning routine* is simple.

Morning Routine
- •Time with the Lord.
- •Make bed promptly.
- •Shower.
- •Get fully dressed.
- •Check accumulation spots (explanation following).
- •Tidy each room.
- •Drink three glasses of water and have light breakfast.
- •Empty Dishwasher (I've found this somewhat dreaded task takes all of 5 minutes).
- •Do ten-minute room routine (explanation following).
- •Check email.

After this I'm free to do my daily list for the day.

Daily Routines

It's beneficial for me to have scheduled days for many of my routine jobs. I do laundry on *Monday* and *Thursday*. The cleaning gets done on *Wednesday*, and groceries are purchased on *Friday*. This is what my *daily routines* page consists of. If I wake up on a Tuesday and haven't made my daily list the night before, I can refer to this page and my mind is enlightened.

Monday	**Tuesday**	**Wednesday**
Devotions	Devotions	Devotions
Ten min. room	Ten min. room	Ten min.room
Laundry	Iron	Clean
Upload site	Christa	Market book
Writing	Guests	Call one lady
Note to Bob		

Thursday	**Friday**	**Saturday**
Devotions	Devotions	Devotions
Ten min.room	Ten min.room	Ten min.room
Laundry	Town	Baking
Writing	Market book	Market book
Type sermon	Visiting	
	Guests	

Your *daily routines* will be different than mine. I saw my daughter's list a few days ago. She's a young mother and it listed mothering items. (e.g. 10:00 story time).

Ten-minute Room Routine

I love my *ten-minute room routine* cleaning lists. I can keep my cleaning under control if I take just ten minutes a day with one room in my house, during my *morning routine*.

> Every job is a self-portrait of the person who does it. Autograph your work with excellence.

I listed the rooms in my home and divided them up so they fit into a three week period. That means one room will get ten minutes of careful attention one day each month. This is in addition to my weekly cleaning.

I begin the **first** week of the month. On **Monday** I do the master bathroom; I check the cupboards and drawers to make sure no stash or clutter has collected, (tidying up those places takes about 30 seconds) look around for cobwebs or extra dust, wipe the cupboard fronts and that room is done. On **Tuesday**, it is time for the master bedroom; in this room I tidy the closet and remove clothes that are no longer used, check for webs and straighten up the contents of the drawers. On **Wednesday** I move to the living room; where I tidy the closet, remove anything in the room that has collected and check for those pesky webs. On **Thursday**, I'm in the spare bedroom; again I do the routine checks: Tidy in the closet, drawers and check for webs. On **Friday**, I tackle the big bathroom.

The **second Monday** of the month I start in the office doing my *ten-minute round* there. That **Tuesday** is the kitchen. **Wednesday**, I'm in the dining room. On **Thursday** the laundry rooms gets ten minutes of my time and **Friday**, it's the basement kitchen.

On **Monday** of week **three** I start in the basement pantry, **Tuesday** it's the basement spare room and **Wednesday** the basement storage room. **Thursday** is the day I run through the bathroom downstairs, and **Friday** I work in the family room.

> You can endure or enjoy most anything for 10 minutes.

Since all of my rooms fit into a three week slot I take off the **last** week of the month with *ten-minute routines*. On the **first Monday** of the next month I start back in again. It's amazing to me that things stay so neatly in order by taking ten short minutes of time in each room, once each month. If I happen to miss a day I'll catch it with next month's cleaning.

For my bigger monthly undertakings, in **February** every year on the proper day for each room, I use my schmopp (wall mop) to do the walls, and I vacuum the carpet edges. In **March** and **October** the curtains and insides of the windows get washed, and I dust down the furniture. I wash the curtains for several rooms together to save water. In **April** the light bulbs and fixtures are washed for my *ten-minute routine* in each room. **April** and **November** is when the wall hangings get cleaned with Windex.

With the routine list in the miscellaneous section, I have no excuse not to remember what room I need to do each day and each month. I check the list at the beginning of each week and transfer the right room to my *daily list* page. If you think in terms of ten minutes a day, housecleaning doesn't feel so overwhelming.

Accumulation Spots

Another routine I like to keep high in my mind every day is my *accumulation spots*. Do you know what these are? Mine happen to be; my dining room table, the kitchen bar, the counter top beside the refrigerator, the coffee table in the living room and the desks in the office. Without thinking I leave *papers* and *stuff* lay in these spots until the whole house appears messy. I've gotten into a habit each morning and evening to check these *accumulation spots* and clean them up. It takes only a couple of minutes if I do it habitually twice a day.

My friend who still has children at home, tells me her children are each responsible for two of the *accumlation spots* in their home. They straighten up those places twice a day.

Eliminate Routine

If you're a collector, maybe you need to address this issue. We are surrounded by a world of *stuff* and it uses up way too much of our precious time.

Learn to *eliminate*. Keep a wastebasket and a used item box in several rooms of your home. Use them regularly every day. As soon as you get the mail sort through it. Put each item in its home and throw away every thing that is not needed. Do not stack it up to go through later. When you purchase a new item of clothing check to see if something else needs eliminated. If you find something, put it into the used item box promptly. Anything you discover during your *ten-minute room routine* that is no longer used needs to be either thrown away or placed in the used box.

If you're really deep in *stuff* at your house, consider getting rid of a bagful each Thursday afternoon. Address one room per week shoving 20 unused items into your bag. Don't ponder the items long, and don't consider the contents once they are in the bag. Quickly remove the bag from your house to the car, never to return. It takes three extra minutes to drop off the bag at the local used store during your weekly town trip.

Stuff creates chaos and chaos causes confusion. We need to be cleaned out and clutter free to feel rested, relaxed and at peace in our homes.

Home Routine
　　Everything needs a place to live and things need to belong somewhere. Similar to the way we enjoy returning to our dwelling place at the end of a long day. After using an item I try to immediately place it back in its home. If I find a particular thing has no home, I find it one. It will stay there until it's needed another time. My rule is, a place for everything and everything in it's place.
　　Although my children are now grown and away from home. I know most of these routines can be accomplished even in a house filled with lively children. As children grow they become helpful instruments in routines. Each child's name can be placed beside several jobs on our routine lists.
　　I've followed this type of routine living ever since my daughters were tiny. It certainly does eliminate the confusion that can often invade our homes.
　　Discipline is the name of the game when it comes to sticking to the routines and lists each day until everything is done. Procrastination generally doesn't fit into a good homemaking plan. After the jobs are crossed off, there is the opportunity for free time, an activity of our choice or a ministry project with the children.
　　Don't forget though, just as the planner idea does not fit Bob, it may not be for you either. One of my daughters finds she doesn't need a planner at this stage in her life. Another daughter is a big time organizer/notebooker. Her two-year-old daughter, Sierra, is extremely careful, meticulous and neat. She loves her mommy's notebook. Her mother found an inexpensive planner much like her own, gave it to Sierra and she certainly uses it. My other daughter uses her planner off and on. You may have another method for managing your time and keeping your lists that works better for you and that's ok.

Finger Prints

Hope Byler, 2003

A little dust here
a cobweb clings there—
daily dirt, daily fuzzies—
a family thrives here . . .
sacred duties,
those excursions
of "capture the spider" . . .
acts of worship—
to tidy, to scrub,
so as to bless my family
with peaceful surroundings.

As I dust off
little fingerprints
left behind by the inquisitive,
my heart sings a prayer
that in my children
would blossom
the wide-eyed wonder
of discovering —
in THEIR everyday routines —
fingerprints of God.

Follow the Path of Jesus

Christopher Ruby Blackall, 1830

Follow the path of Jesus,
Walk where His footsteps lead;
Keep in His beaming presence,
Every counsel heed;
Watch, while the hours are flying,
Ready some good to do;
Quick, while His voice is calling,
Yield obedience true!

Cling to the hand of Jesus,
All through the day and night;
Dark though the way and dreary,
He will guide you right.
Live for the good of others,
Helpless, oppressed and wrong;
Lift them from depths of sorrow,
In His strength be strong!

Take up the cross of Jesus,
Sharing the shame He bore;
Self and the world denying,
Love the Saviour more;
Tell all the world of Jesus,
Think of their gloom and loss,
Tell of His great salvation,
Glory in His cross.

6

"If God Wills"

*A*as I mentioned, we do our planning under the umbrella of *"If God wills."* I planned my day sometime ago as usual. My list went like this:

- •Devotions.
- •One hour on computer.
- •Groceries.
- •Visit Mary.
- •Market my books.
- •Dinner preparations.

Before I left for groceries, however, Christa phoned. She and the children wanted to get out of the house, "Could they come over for the morning?" I'm always pleased to have my family with me, so I said, "Sure."

Replanning my day, I decided I would go for groceries in the afternoon.

Minutes after Christa arrived, I received a phone call from my friend Kris. She urgently wondered if I could come to her house. A young mother had just stopped by and wanted to take her own life. Kris felt weak spiritually and desired my help. Christa accustomed to my running at any moment, (having been with us in Christian ministry most of her life) accepted the interruption as usual, and I went to my friend.

> A quiet joy comes when we live the way God calls us to live.
>
> *John Yates*

The encounter with Kris' friend turned out to be crucial. I laid hands on this young woman and her husband, and prayed fervently for them. Remembering my son-in-law's Bible in the van, I retrieved it and gave it to the woman. Although she was heavily involved in satanic readings, when I placed the Bible in her hands, she was thrilled, repeating, "This is what I need, this is what I need." Within the course of the few minutes I spent with her, I witnessed a dramatic change in her spirit. As she prepared to leave, she thanked me profusely. The couple and their three small children drove away and I blessed the Lord for detours. Returning home, I enjoyed my grandbabies until Christa took them home.

I was getting ready to leave the house for the afternoon grocery trip when the phone rang again. This was Rhonda who is Alina's mother. Twelve years ago, Alina lived with us in foster care for most of her first year of life. Rhonda was concerned about an upcoming event and wanted to talk. We visited for awhile, prayed together over the phone and laid her burden at the cross.

One more time I prepared to go for groceries. The phone rang yet again. This time Marie, the hospice nurse, was calling to discuss plans for a lady at the nursing home.

You know, I didn't get my list finished that day. There would be another time to purchase groceries. The Lord's plan for me held a different list than mine. I've learned if I do my work, my lists, my jobs "as unto the Lord," I do not become overwhelmed or emotionally distraught when there are changes to my plan. If I do the work for myself or "as unto men," interruptions can cause eruptions in my spirit.

It's very important for us to live under the umbrella of *"If God wills"* and do all we do "as unto Him."

Teach me to do your will, for you are my God;.
May your good Spirit lead me on level ground.

Psalm 143:10

Silent Night

Joseph Mohr, 1818

Silent Night! Holy Night!
All is calm, all is bright,
Round yon virgin, mother and Child;
Holy Infant, so tender and mild,
Sleep in heavenly peace, Sleep in heavenly peace.

Silent night! Holynight!
Shepherds quake at the site!
Glories stream from heaven afar,
Heavenly hosts sing alleluia.
Christ, the Saviour, is born! Christ, the Savior is born.

Silent night! Holy night! Son of God, love's pure light.
Radiant beams from Thy holy face,
With the dawn of redeeming grace,
Jesus, Lord, at Thy birth,
Jesus, Lord, at Thy birth.

7

A Peaceful December

$\mathcal{E}$ach of us are seeking to honor the Lord as our priority relationship in life. As Christmas approaches I use a few organizational methods to help free my energies for more important things. If I follow these ideas I have more time to focus specifically on Christ, the greatest *gift of love*. If you celebrate the Lord's first coming, you might enjoy taking a peek at my ideas. I like to have everything prepared for the celebration by the end of the first week in December.

1. The first week of November is a great time to address the cards or letters I send as messages of love to those far and near. My letter gets written right after Thanksgiv-

ing. Everything is ready to drop into the mailbox by the first of December.

2. I enjoy giving a few *gifts* as a token of love at this time of year. At the beginning of each year I write down the names of everyone I'd like to buy gifts for. This list is the last page in the *shopping list* section of my planner. Throughout the year when I hear someone mention something they would like, I jot that down under their name. At the end of October I spend time carefully, prayerfully considering a gift for each person on my list. I like to be sure I'm passing along a gift that is in tune with the message of my heart.

As I mentioned, clutter creates confusion. It's the same for our children. Children don't do well with an over abundance of toys.

Checking on useful things such as clothing needs helps to eliminate clutter. I find this is better than spend-ing excessive amounts of money on unnecessary items. Sometimes the need is socks or boots. Other times one needs a winter coat or a sweater.

Along with the clothing, a useful toy can com-plete the *gift of love* for each child. I try to steer away from the latest, expensive electronic items. Children do well with puzzles, books and table games. They're great for encouraging good memory, thinking and focusing pro-cesses. Since my granddaughter, Sierra, was 18 month old, she's regularly spent 45-minutes at a time amongst a pile of books. She goes from one to the next, learning all along the way. In fact, Sierra often sits for 30-minutes studying my book *Treasures From a Mother's Heart*??? I certainly don't know what a baby learns from it, but she has the pictures and the names to each one memorized.

3. As grandmas, it's important to be wise in our spending at Christmas time. We can set a godly example by being careful.

I love to make snuggly pajamas for my grandbabies each year and get a useful item to go with them. Some grandparents start a savings account with a $10.00 bill for each child. They add another ten-dollars next Christmas and the next. My grandma gave a very nice book to each of the great grandchildren at Christmas for many years.

> God's gifts put man's best dream's to shame.
>
> *Elizabeth Barrett Browning*

4. For adult gifts, a basket filled with perishable items is one of my favorites. Crackers, cheese spreads, fruits and cookies are great to have when sharing the *gift of friendship* over the holidays.

5. In early November I like to take a shopping day to purchase my listed items. This saves me from impulsive spending. It also cuts down on the hustle of December, and days' worth of shopping time. It's important to me to have everything purchased by November 20. Each gift can be wrapped and tucked away well before December.

6. I prepare and plan to do my Christmas baking and candy making the first week of December. Most cookies and treats can be done early and hidden in the freezer or

under a bed. At our house this has been the practice for many years. However, each year when I go to collect these prepared foods on the day I want them, sneaky fingers have found their way to the tucked away boxes. There are usually a few treats missing. It's become a family fun activity by now. Often those last couple of weeks before Christmas I'll see someone wandering through the house, finally they're saying, "Well, *where* are they this year??" (My son-in-law is especially noted for this.)

7. Bob and I often look for a family in need that we can purchase *love gifts* for. When the girls lived at home we all traveled to town one evening to pick out the gifts. We had a great time packaging everything into a box, praying together for the family and sending the bundle off.

That's my plan for enjoying the twelfth month of the year. I know the Lord is blessed by our fellowship and sharing as we celebrate His birth each year. And He's deeply honored when we take the time to quiet ourselves before Him in rest and worship during this special time as well.

How silently, how silently,
the wondrous gift is given!

Phillip Brooks
(O Little town of Bethlehem)

8

Organizational Tips

𝓘n bringing this book to a close, I'll share with you a few miscellaneous tips I've found helpful through the years. The more compact and carefully we live our lives, the more time we have left in our days to sit with the Father, and to minister for Him. Remember that's our purpose for being on this earth.

1. I like to keep my addresses organized in a notebook from A - Z. Immediately when a new or changed address arrives, it's important for me to update the book.

2. I think of the two words *"avoid clutter"* wherever I'm working. If there is something I'm not using at the moment, it needs cleared away. Whether I'm cooking in the kitchen or working in the office, the counter and desk

tops should be available for just what I'm working on. Items should be in their homes and papers in their files. It generally takes only a little time to clear away a job before getting the next one out.

3. It's important for me to keep my recipe box in order. After I use a recipe I'm tempted to stick the card in the cupboard to file later. I've learned this is not a good habit. I remind myself to re-file my recipe immediately behind the proper food group tab.

4. When my girls grew up and left home I found I did not keep up with photo albums, plus we have so many of those bulky books. I got myself a shoe box size plastic storage box. Then I made and dated divider cards that were a little larger than the photos with the years' dates I needed. (1990, 1991, 1992, etc.) Now I keep the pictures for the right year neatly in place behind the dated divider. The pictures remain in order and are available to be enjoyed. Over the years I've learned it's very important to date my pictures the day I get them back from the developer.

> I want you to smile when you look around your home. Everything that you own should bring you joy.
>
> *FlyLady*

5. A storage tub works great for appliance manuals and warranties.

6. When my girls were young I used cardboard boxes to store out-grown clothing. Today my daughters have the easy-to-use plastic storage tubs. Each tub is labeled with sizes, (ie: boys 3-6 months; girls 18 months-2 years) When one grows out of something the item gets placed in the right tub. It's a great way to have clothing for the next size readily available.

7. I enjoy using plastic storage boxes for Christmas decorations, extra blankets, pillows, financial business or anything that needs stashed away.

Storage boxes stack well. I've found it's helpful to number my boxes and keep a list of the numbers in my notebook. The contents of each box is written beside the number. It's an easy way to find what I'm looking for. It works best if the numbered label on the boxes face toward me when I enter the storage room!

8. It's not best to store items for years on end. In fact, a good plan for me, is to keep only one of each thing in my house. I had to ask myself why do I have four can openers? Certainly, one is all I need. It's the same for many other household things. An age old habit to keep current is, if I don't use something for one year, give it another home.

Dear friends, each of us are designed by the hand of God, called to fulfill a special purpose. He desires for us to take some time to hear His voice, trust His plan, organize our lives to free us to move ahead connecting our people groups to Him. May He be glorified by our lives.

Your Friend

Donna Kauffman

Let your eyes look directly ahead,
And let your gaze be fixed straight in front of you.
Watch the path of your feet,
And all your ways will be established.
Do not turn to the right nor to the left;
Turn your foot from evil.

Proverbs 4:25-27

About the Author

Donna Kauffman is the mother of three grown daughters—Carla, Rachel and Christa—Grandmother of three, Kyle, Sierra and Kassie. Donna and her husband, Bob live in Parkman, Ohio where he is the pastor at Agape Mennonite Church and a Corian countertop salesman. As a couple they enjoy ministering to families. When Donna's not busy sharing with her children and grandchildren, she finds herself encouraging mothers and grandmothers. Donna leads Bible studies, makes baby blankets and sews for the grandchildren. She even squeezes in time for speaking engagements and writing. Donna has one other book titled, *Treasures From a Mother's Heart—A Celebration of Memories From One Generation to Another*, and a free monthly email newsletter, *Treasures From My Heart to Yours*.

For more information about Donna's books, to sign up for her newsletter, or to share how God has used this book in your life, please write to Donna at:

Donna Kauffman
19151 Hobart Road
West Farmington, Ohio 44491

Phone: 440-548-5436
Email: treasures@djkauffman.com
www.djkauffman.com.